A LIVING ISLAND

Ireland's responsibility to nature

MICHAEL VINEY

D1353794

COMHAR
THE NATIONAL
SUSTAINABLE
DEVELOPMENT
PARTNERSHIP

2003

*'Just as a country treasures its finite historical episodes,
classic books, works of art, and other measures of national greatness,
it should learn to treasure its unique and finite ecosystems,
resonant to a sense of time and place.'*
—EDWARD O. WILSON, The Diversity of Life.[1]

T HE LAST WINTER SNOW OF 2000 was ushered off the
mountains by a rain-laden gale from the Atlantic, reducing
their brief Alpine glory to a profile of wet hessian. A few white
shreds hung on in the distant cliff of the Sheeffrys and that
summoned the desolation I knew to exist on the slopes below: a
slick, black desert, stubbled with scant tufts of sedge and wiry
mat-grass, glistening with rivulets running with peat-silt. 'The
bog's final break-up into black mush is a shocking thing to see' I
had written in January 1994, and for all the subsequent efforts to
reduce sheep numbers on the hills and the plans for the
management of shared upland commonages, ecological disaster is
still plain. In places it is beyond repair: an entire fabric of
vegetation, from heather and *Molinia* moorgrass to leafy
liverworts and mosses, shorn away by relentless overgrazing.

It took a couple of decades for a bad policy decision to show
up on the ground – the first years, as it happened, of my own
family's switch to country living. Our farming neighbours were
first to point out the slow black bruises darkening on the slopes,
the plume of peat silt spreading from the estuary after rain. Soon
there were changes in the sheep as well, a certain gaunt lack of
substance beneath the fleece as torrents of ewes were rushed
along the road to be counted past the headage inspector.

The decision-making that produced this degradation was a

I

classic of unsustainable development. The idea was well-meant: a regional subsidy on ewes to encourage lamb production by small hill-farmers in 'disadvantaged' areas. But it was born of a mechanistic picture of farming, a construct of near-abstract inputs and outputs, which left nature entirely out of account. The carrying capacity of fragile, nutrient-poor peatland was of a totally different order to grassland on lowland mineral soil.

If this did not occur to the EU agronomists, it should certainly have been the concern of Ireland's own experts. But only when the damage became scandalous and undeniable was the grazing impact on blanket bog vegetation suddenly worth studying. As for the hill farmers, years of conditioning to a sense of marginal worth, if not, indeed, of being a final generation of their kind, did nothing to encourage wise use of the land. In this demoralised mood, the mountain commonage became a 'wasteland' and its future lost all meaning.

When the notion of 'sustainable development' is applied to landscape and its natural plants and animals, values tend to swing about between aesthetics (the appreciation of beauty, and pleasure to our senses) which is largely shaped by human culture, and attitudes arising from the science of ecology. We have travelled beyond simple responses to the scent of a flower, the song of a bird, to a new understanding of context: a bird now becomes 'rare', a flowering meadow a 'threatened habitat'.

Aesthetic judgments are notoriously subjective and tastes have changed with time. My own keen enjoyment of the 'untamed', rocky landscape that surrounds Killary Harbour, and of the wild weather that so often sweeps through it, has cultural roots in the Romantic movement of the eighteenth century. Before that, a 'beautiful' landscape was that made by man – cornfields and orchards – and Connemara was a vision of nature at its most uncontrolled and threatening. There was no science of ecology to inspire the Romantic movement of philosophers, painters and writers, but their intuitions helped to restore human confidence in the relationship with nature, in belonging to the Earth as one species among the rest.

The supposed 'subjectivity' of tastes in landscape and of deciding what is beautiful has created all kinds of problems for decision-makers, who feel helpless without the framework of numbers and boxes. But issues of ecology, too, are often overlaid with ambivalence and confusion. Why, first of all, should we bother with the conservation of species, with 'biodiversity'? Ninety-nine per cent of the species that have ever existed are extinct, yet the evolution of life has furnished the planet with more species today than at any other period; as we peer minutely into the Earth's interstices, we are discovering new ones all the time. Even if human activities have launched a crisis of extinctions which threatens to compare with global cataclysms of fire and ice, where is its real significance?

At the most popular level, there is the instinctive pleasure in nature's variety, at least in its familiar and colourful forms. The notion that this should be handed on intact 'to our grandchildren' is now a moral imperative for many people. Quite as appealing to utilitarian minds is the wisdom of keeping the maximum number of species up humanity's sleeve for potential future use: a pool of genes for new crop species; a cure for cancer in the rainforest.

We may think also, or instead, that we need a full range of species to sustain the planet's natural equilibrium, for the incidental but fortunate benefit of human life. The idea of the whole Earth running itself as a living organism (the 'Gaia' of the British scientist James Lovelock)[2] remains an unprovable hypothesis, but one that steadily gains scientific support. With it spreads a new appreciation of the way species work together in ecosystems, with global warming as an ultimate demonstration that 'everything connects to everything else'. We may not be 'threatening the planet' (another, if unwitting, piece of hubris) but we could affect Earth's systems in ways that make our own survival very uncomfortable

One option is to accept – as I do – that other species and their habitats have an intrinsic claim or 'right' to exist which is independent of the interests of human beings. In philosophical terms this is a tricky one, since 'rights' can scarcely exist outside a human value system. Much of the intuitive support for the idea comes from rejection of biblical teachings that seemed to award man a mastery over nature and even a duty to subdue and exploit other species. This kind of language may have ebbed from the modern Christian tradition, but its assumptions still run strongly through our culture.

For example, the Green 2000 Advisory Group, set up by Charles Haughey and reporting in 1993, decided that 'nature conservation may be defined as the sustainable use of nature'. [3] 'Use', in this context, may have been meant benignly, but it is typical of attitudes that perpetuate a gulf between people and their fellow species. Only a deeper awareness of our place *within* nature can help reinstate *Homo sapiens* in the balance and health of Earth's essential processes (most urgently, at this time, the planet's carbon cycle). It is what should dictate our concern for the vanishing Amazonian forests and the integrity of the oceans. It should decide what sort of wastes we create, how we recycle the Earth's resources (as nature does) and how we limit our population to match them.

In our small and well-worn island, all the natural ecosystems have already been heavily modified and compromised. There is scarcely a footfall of land that hasn't been dug up, built on or grazed for centuries: even our few fragments of wildwood show the coppiced trunks of ancient husbandry. Indeed, what we think of as our wildest country is often the most abused. Unlike Americans, for example, who really do have some wilderness left, the only relatively unscathed territory we can choose to leave alone lies beneath our Atlantic coastal waters. The future of our terrestrial landscape will continue to be shaped by the sum of human decisions. And in so far as these consciously relate to conservation, they will amount to 'stewardship' and even human 'management'.

The close of the twentieth century produced a scientific specialism known as 'restoration ecology', bringing back degraded habitats to something like their former richness and stability. In trials in Killarney National Park, for example, local Kerry cattle have been reintroduced to the hills in summer, in place of sheep – a grazing regime that emulates the 'booleying' (transhumance) practised in pre-twentieth-century Ireland. They are wintered in paddocks which are closed off in autumn to allow the vegetation to grow. Both measures have improved the health and diversity of the plant life. At the same time, a conservation plant nursery in the park has been raising tree and shrub stock for planting trials on the hills. It includes Scots pine, a tree probably extinct on Irish uplands since medieval times, together with 'lost' dwarf shrubs such as juniper and cowberry, with berries important to birds and mammals. [4]

The first concern, logically, is the restoration of the national parks, from Killarney to Connemara, north Mayo to Donegal. Some parts may be left to nature's own time for shrub and tree regeneration and even closed to people entirely. But an ecological formula that found a place for human husbandry could also be used to restore great tracts of Ireland's upland commonage, especially those fringed by farmers already adapting to management plans within the Rural Environment Protection Scheme (REPS). Some ecologists would argue that such 'environmental manipulation' (even 'wildlife gardening') would be absurdly costly, and that if reafforestation is the objective, then moorland should simply be fenced off and left to nature. But the reintroduction of Kerry cattle, a small but hardy, dual-purpose breed with an appetite for moorgrass, would introduce a fresh dimension. Keeping 'Kerries' fits happily into organic farming and would allow the hills to grow back many of their lost plants. In the meantime, limiting the sheep should see the slow return of heathers and sedge, if not the shrubs whose seed banks have dwindled and died out, and the Atlantic mosses and liverworts that once grew beneath them.

In the lowland countryside, the steady loss of species should be slowed or even reversed in the changes brought about by the Rural Environment Protection Scheme, co-funded by Europe and the state. By the turn of the century the scheme embraced some 43,000 farmers, most of them with holdings of less than 40 hectares (100 acres). They will be joined by many thousands more – generally the countryside of high ecological value – where subsidies to livestock have been changed to direct payments based on land.

Along with limits to stock numbers and the use of chemical fertilizer, REPS pays farmers to follow management plans that recognise both aesthetic and ecological goals. Hedges are important to wildlife, but also 'give the Irish landscape its distinctive character and field pattern'. Stone walls protect wildlife as well as stock, and merit repair and maintenance as 'an important element in the landscape'. Colours and materials of farm and outbuildings should be 'sympathetic to traditions of country building'. The ecological measures are detailed and far-reaching, but sit within a broadly ideal visual image of a small-farm countryside that took on its shape in the first fifty years of the twentieth century.

The decision to conserve and restore the appearance of such a countryside, with its small-scale, irregular weave of walls, hedges and copses, its relatively intimate connection between people and livestock, clearly reflects the urban culture of elite committees, as well as the middle-class choices of tourism. This can seem like a city-bred nostalgia for a range of archaic rural images now quite unsustainable on working farms. But the way in which intuitive, well-educated taste corresponds with good practice in ecological conservation is more than a coincidence. Farm landscape with great diversity of vegetation, field boundaries that offer good cover, open ditches and waterways, odd corners of deliberate 'neglect', are simply richer in species than intensively ordered rye-grass pastures partitioned by wire fences. Indeed, it is likely that, in post-glacial Ireland, the peak of habitat diversity and richness of species existed, not in the canopied primal forests, but in the countryside of small, mixed farms of less than a century ago.

A study published in 1999[5] of small farms at Annaghdown, beside Lough Corrib, County Galway, as they were run in the 1940s, showed the remarkable diversity within the farm as well as in the landscape itself, which still kept its turloughs and callows, woodland and limestone scrub. It was farming without tractors or artificial fertilizers and managed for a family life with a minimum of bought-in food. The farmers kept Shorthorn and Hereford cattle, Galway ewes, Clydesdale and Irish draught horses, Large White and Landrace pigs, four or five breeds of hens and assorted ducks, geese and turkeys. The crops were oats, wheat, barley, potatoes, mangolds and turnips, and sugar beet for the factory in Tuam. Each group of crops, each kind of livestock, created particular niches for insects, birds and small mammals, even tillage 'weeds' such as cornflower and corn marigold, now virtually extinct in Ireland. The loss of mixed farming has cost us the corn bunting, brought the corncrake and grey partridge close to extinction, and made the yellowhammer a rarity across much of the island.

The study was intended to see what wisdom traditional farming systems might offer (in stocking densities, grazing seasons and so on) for the management of conservation, especially of wildlife habitats included in REPS farms. But I find it striking that ecological science, seeking a model balance between farming and biodiversity, should focus upon the landscapes of mixed farming which are now so widely treasured as aesthetically satisfying. This does, of course, invite the question of the accompanying lifestyle. The Annaghdown farms lived to a low-income pattern of subsistence, further shaped by

7

wartime shortages. Who would want to live like that today?

It takes a radical green economist like Mayo's Richard Douthwaite to analyse the illusion that industrialised, high-input farming creates the highest value.[6] But a very positive endorsement of localised mixed-farm systems already comes from authentically organic farmers (by 'authentic' I mean people who have come to organic farming through personal understanding and conviction, not those who merely conform to minimum disciplines in return for improved grants or prices). The genuine article feels part of a movement or philosophy aimed at working with nature, enriching the soil and conserving wildlife. Species diversity, planting of broadleaf trees, using animal manures – these become positive ends in themselves. And while the revolution in consumer attitudes has brought quite unexpected rewards to many organic farmers and growers, their first impetus, often in retreat from city stresses, was far from material and was concerned with the quality of life.

There are now quite a lot of people in Ireland, the UK and Europe for whom such a lifestyle, with its keen ecological sense, would offer great fulfilment. At the same time, much 'disadvantaged' land in Ireland (to use a convenient term) is held by semi-retired or part-time farmers. Many of them have lost all real engagement with agriculture, but retain their satisfaction with country living. Over wide areas, participation in REPS will come down to a modest flock of sheep, easily manageable in spare time, and as large a plantation of conifer forestry as the REPS planner will allow.

The sale of sites for holiday homes, especially in scenic areas, will be an extra pressure on land which has lost its traditional function, and will probably continue to inflate its price. Away from areas of major development or expanding intensive farms, it seems unlikely that much land will find its way to the market. The symbolic value of land ownership is still powerful and has kept many 'empty' small farms, together with their houses, within extended families. Nonetheless, support for a progressive transfer of farmland in areas of high ecological value to committed organic farmers (perhaps by secure leaseholds with initial grant assistance) could work to restore lost biodiversity and keep farming active within an aesthetically pleasing landscape.

'Farmers have traditionally been the guardians of the countryside and its heritage. They are aware of the importance of protecting the natural environment, both in its own right and as the resource base for their livelihood....' Such sentiments (here from *Sustainable Development: A Strategy for Ireland*)[7] are a familiar national piety, not always warranted. The practices and attitudes of Ireland's farmers have been substantially shaped by government research, advisory services and farming media, all heavily influenced by a technical culture of intensive production, chemical inputs and ever-more-elaborate machines. Concern for the natural environment, where it exists, has been partly an assimilative process – as, indeed, it has been for most people – and often a forced response to immediate problems of pollution. What most farmers know of nature, in the ecological sense, is just as likely to derive from watching wildlife films on television as from watching actual birds or insects in the field. An exception must, of course, be made for the substantial number of farmers who are lifelong hunters and do at least appreciate the relationship of the quarry and habitat.

Ecology is often now so 'scientific' and far removed from the casual observation of nature that the balance of environment with farming practice will probably continue to be led by expert advice and example. But this need not always mean hi-tech solutions – perhaps even the opposite. County Waterford has seen, for example, in the Anne Valley, the highly successful operation of a 'constructed' wetland. It links a series of planted reedbeds and pools so that polluted farmyard water ends up pure enough for trout to live in. Similar 'made' wetlands are purifying rural sewage and absorbing toxic minerals from mining. Their widespread adoption would create substantial new habitats for wildlife, of the kind so widely destroyed by the drainage schemes of the past.

The arterial drainage of Ireland, which reached its peak in the 1970s and '80s, was an engineers' crusade in the service of agriculture. In almost forty river catchments, riverbeds were brutally dredged into a U-shape, the banks clawed back to the steepest angle the local clays would sustain. Spoil was dumped into nearby ponds and marshes, or left heaped on the banks like miners' waste. The ecological devastation was severe, and not merely for the short term. In Britain, similar excesses produced a powerful reaction among ecologists[8] and a far-reaching change in the engineers' approach to the natural life of a river and its tributaries. In Ireland, a new engineering regime has been brought to all the rivers managed by the Office of Public Works. It allows them, for example, a naturally asymmetrical bed, creating 'hydraulic diversity' and trout-friendly habitats.

In the prime trout and salmon catchments of the west, regional fisheries boards have gone a lot further in restoring lowland streams dug out in the drainage schemes of the 1960s. They have brought back the natural 'valley' that streams carve in their beds, and natural sequences of riffle, glide and pool; they have created willow-shade, and hollows beneath the banks for fish to hide. To follow these waterways now is to see birds and insects that had vanished from the barren gutters of the drainage schemes, and to hear the water-music of a living stream. Once again it seems that habitats which please the human senses are also those that nature fills with life.

A decade ago, the construction company ESB International was given the contract to reconstruct the derelict and overgrown Ballinamore-Ballyconnell Canal, fifty kilometres long and linking Ireland's two great waterways, the Shannon and the Erne. As a development for leisurely, waterborne tourism, supported by the EU's Regional Development Fund, it warranted special ecological care. Before a rock was drilled or a tree-trunk lopped, the company brought in ecologists to survey the wildlife of the canal and its lakes, rivers and marshes. Their brief kept habitat destruction to a minimum on every yard of waterway (the diggers, for example, working from one bank only, or even from rafts, to leave long stretches of bank, with their trees and herbage, intact). Today, the canal is one of the loveliest of its kind in these islands, with wildlife of a richness unequalled in a century.

Slowly, nature is claiming its place on agendas at a level that cannot be ignored. In the EU's new Water Framework Directive, now the concern of Irish hydrologists, geographers, drainage engineers, environmental scientists and planners, each river basin will have to be managed so that there is enough good water for 'sustainable development' of human settlements and industry — but also for all the needs of terrestrial and aquatic ecosystems. With integrated planning and the willingness to think across disciplines, we are less likely to make nature an incidental casualty of change.

It is hard to know how much damage we could have avoided decades ago. Even if the science existed, our thought for nature did not. All around me, in the mountain valleys of Mayo and Connemara, the conifer forests were planted right up to the banks of rivers and across the streams that fed them. As the trees grew up, they shut out the sunlight from riparian insect-life. Peat silt from the forest drains flowed down to choke the spawning-grounds of salmon and trout. In the uplands, the conifers helped to tip the acid balance of the water against aquatic invertebrates, the food for fish, so that stream after stream began to die.

Today we know better. The forests have withdrawn behind broad buffer zones and leave the riverbanks open to the sun. Margins of moorgrass and scrub complete the river ecosystem with their swarms of insects.

Looking back, it seems impossible we could ever not have realised that farm and forestry fertilizer and domestic sewage, running off into our lakes and rivers, would produce the fatal over-nourishment we have learned to call 'eutrophication'. Today, the insidious inflow of phosphorus is slowly falling back, but its accumulative damage persists. It can be seen in the decline of such sensitive species as the Arctic char (*Salvelinus alpinus*), which arrived in Ireland's rivers with the salmon and trout ten thousand years ago, and the freshwater pearl mussel (*Margaritifera margaritifera*), which, left in peace, can live for a century.

The conservation of species in Ireland has not, alas, been founded on any strong, indigenous concern. As a political and economic society, we only yesterday woke up to what science might do for us. As for what it ought to be doing for nature, the number of ecologists in regular work outside the universities could, until ten or twenty years ago, be counted on one's fingers. I have yet to meet any of them who would argue with the species and habitats listed in the various EU conservation directives (making the various surveys has, after all, been good for professional business). But on a broader front, the lack of Irish discussion of the content of the directives shows how modest was our capacity to do more than simply carry them out.

These directives, as the consensus of a European scientific elite, are having a considerable impact on national land-use policies and individual livelihoods. They have set the priorities for conservation of biodiversity, for which future generations will, one hopes, be grateful. Without it, the island's landscape would have been at the mercy of the great surge of economic development and construction which arrived with the new century.

It is sad, however, that the whole conservation apparatus of Natural Heritage Areas (NHAs), the Special Areas of Conservation (SACs) selected from them, and the Special Protection Areas (SPAs) for birds, has been presented to a rural society generally so ill-equipped to see their point. What has the protection of snails and plants almost too small to see, or of 'ugly' parasites like lampreys (which merit no fewer than five SACs), got to do with people's real lives? They are 'threatened' or they are 'rare': so what – who needs them, other than scientists pursuing their own peculiar agenda?

The fact that such species are generally found surviving in vestiges of semi-natural landscape which also make good scenery has introduced some confusion in the public mind – perhaps fortunately, since looking after the scenery is a social and economic value which is widely understood. It has also helped people to accept the idea of Special Areas of Conservation, and to accept the list of a representative range of 'important' habitats which were designated as SACs – Ireland's contribution to Europe's Natura 2000 network. Bog and fen, limestone pavement, turloughs, machair dunes, Atlantic oakwoods, salmon rivers, trout lakes – these are so distinctive of the Irish landscape and so obviously likely to have special ecosystems that the only real point of argument has been how much conservation was 'enough'.

Governments across Europe have tried to arrive at some objective norm which is both scientifically conscientious and not foolishly ahead of their neighbours. The reckoning is both financial and political: Ireland's compensation to farmers, for reducing livestock or curtailing land operations, is expected to amount to £20 million annually, but the actual process of site designation has also been politically fraught, given the fears and misunderstandings of (mainly) small landowners.

Site designation has also introduced an unfortunate breakdown of trust between Dúchas and the conservation organisations concerned for biodiversity. A common position of the five main organisations (An Taisce, Irish Wildlife Trust, BirdWatch Ireland, Irish Peatland Conservation Council and Coastwatch Europe) has been that the seriously incomplete knowledge of Ireland's biodiversity frustrates the selection of a properly comprehensive list of sites, and that the total of those proposed by Dúchas is certainly far too few. In 2000 these five submitted a substantial 'shadow' list of extra sites to the EU Commission many of which were later accepted. Some of them were small but significant habitats which, they felt, could provide sustainable 'stepping-stones' between the bigger SACs. These would prevent SACs from becoming isolated refuges of ecological conservation.

The informal diplomacy of Dúchas field staff in sorting out farmers' objections to SAC boundaries on the ground has led to delays which have angered the EU Commission. Among the conservation organisations, it has also fuelled suspicions, rebutted by Dúchas, of less-than-scientific mapping compromises and decisions. The agency has argued that the extra and patient attention to farmers' concerns, sometimes resulting in minor revisions to boundaries, will be rewarded in more solid and sustainable co-operation in the management of SACs.

The difficulty of introducing conservation regimes into Ireland's rural communities has certainly been underestimated by mainly urban-based conservationists. The steady erosion of small-farmer morale in the closing decades of the twentieth century made it no easier to meet the suspicions and fears of landowners. Without the familiar authority of 'Brussels' to justify what was proposed, it is likely that purely Irish initiatives would have met with even greater resistance at local level. The task of assembling land for national parks, and siting their visitor centres, brought some bruising controversy for the Office of Public Works, and later Dúchas. At a landscape symposium in 2000, Dr Alan Craig, Director of National Parks and Wildlife, made it clear that any further proposals for parks would need to emanate, ideally, from the local community, and certainly come complete with general local agreement. [9]

It seems likely, therefore, that Ireland will continue to occupy the lowest place in the tables of the World Conservation Union in the proportion of national territory which is given the strict protection of national parks and nature reserves – one per cent compared with an average of twelve per cent in almost thirty other developed countries. The NHA and SAC designations, unlike those of national parks and nature reserves, leave landowners in place, and are now the conservation measures of choice. They also create buffer zones around the national parks; however, they generate an extensive responsibility of monitoring and management. At the beginning of 2001, the proposed SACs covered close to 1 million hectares: 10 per cent of the Republic's land area (including one per cent for lakes), plus four per cent of marine areas (including for example, the whole of the Shannon Estuary). In the scale of commitment to conservation, this found Ireland comfortably at the middle of the fifteen states of the European Union. The EU Commission, however, responding to the case presented by the conservation organisations, had pressed Dúchas successfully to protect more raised bogs and salmon-river catchments.

There is real danger, however, that the SACs could be left as ecological 'islands' in an inhospitable, humanised landscape of intensive farming, roads and rural suburbia. Most species need room to travel and disperse, to mate and swap genes, to escape from change and disaster. But as landscape is developed, new barriers appear and habitats are fragmented. In small and isolated populations, the loss in genetic variation may eventually bring extinction.

This is why the idea of ecological corridors and stepping-stones has become so important to European conservation strategies. Riverbanks and hedgerows help species to travel; fens, ponds and little woods can help bridge the gaps between refuges. Some European states need to think big, keeping wild regional corridors of forests and mountains to help the migration of wide-ranging mammals, such as wolves. Ireland's rivers are travelled by fish and otters, but the intimate scale of the landscape brings importance to small and local features: particular hedgerows travelled by bats; roadside corridors of heathland where non-flying beetles can take their time as pedestrians; damp meadows with plants needed as the caterpillar-food of particular butterfly colonies. The texture of conservation thus becomes sensitive to quite minor developments in the countryside.

The challenge is to identify and map the essential network of habitats so that they can be taken into account by local authority planners and recognised and respected even at community level. This will enable some of the responsibility for biodiversity to be shared between Dúchas, with its conservation rangers, and the new Heritage Officers working with local authorities. It will give an extra, protective significance to semi-natural landscapes already important to local people and schools. The basic tools for compiling a national ecological Geographic Information System (GIS), with its limitless elaboration of data on computer, are now being developed by a group of Irish ecological consultants. [10]

The scale at which construction engineering decisions become important to nature can be hugely variable. For example, county council maintenance of old stone bridges over streams frequently includes the spraying of liquid cement across the underside of the arch. This can kill the scarce Daubenton's bat (*Myotis daubentonii*) which roosts in bridge crevices and hunts over water; it can also reduce the available nesting-sites for the dipper (*Cinclus cinclus*) and the grey wagtail (*Motacilla cinerea*), two of Ireland's most attractive river birds. At the other end of the scale come the new motorways, cutting great swathes of roadway through the countryside, and road-widening programmes that sweep away semi-natural margins, replacing their diversity and shelter, their irregular micro-habitats, with endlessly uniform verges and slopes.

The new roadside estate does not have to be an ecological desert even to satisfy the engineer's necessary matrix of sightlines, speed and safety. It takes more grassland out of farming monoculture, and offers ample opportunities for creating new wildlife habitats that enrich both nature and the human traveller.

Already, many road authorities are using small native trees and shrubs to create a linear 'woodland edge' that helps to screen the roads, absorb their noise and fit them into the landscape. In some western counties, the building of new stone walls at the roadside should, in time, provide niches for ferns, mosses and lichens: even – without too much cement at the core – decent nesting cavities for field-mice, wrens and stoats. The official *Sustainable Development* strategy document promises 'appropriate tunnels or other crossing points for animals',[11] although it is not yet clear how this is to be given effect.

New grass embankments, verges and central reservations can acquire their own diversity from wind-blown seed, or the germination of seeds long buried in the soil. Flushes of poppies, ox-eye daisies or foxgloves along new carriageways have been stirred up by the roadworks; even 'lost' species such as the cornflower have reappeared here and there. Deliberate large-scale seeding with native wildflowers is an expert and potentially costly affair, but a combination of expert guidance and amateur effort in their harvesting, growing and planting could be a formula for enriching the new grassy roadsides. So many good intentions that occur to road engineers seem to come to grief because of pressures at the construction site. Old hedges vanish overnight, old trees are smoothed out of the way, opportunities are lost for diversity, both visual and biological. Rain flows off the roads in great quantities: why not use it to make wayside wetlands and ponds?

Enhancing biodiversity must be part of our landscape planning, just as conserving it needs measures incorporated into the policies and programmes of many government departments and agencies. This was implicit in Ireland's ratification of the Convention on Biological Diversity in 1996 and shaped the approach to drawing up the National Biodiversity Plan within the Department of Arts, Heritage, Gaeltacht and the Islands. 'It was considered essential,' said a DAHGI report, to secure the involvement of other government departments in the process – a plan based solely on the work of the government department with responsibility for nature conservation would be considerably different and more limited than one which dealt with all aspects of biodiversity.'[12]

The Department of Agriculture, for example, faces new responsibilities in conserving genetic resources. Having promoted a virtual monoculture of perennial rye-grass and white clover over vast areas of farm grassland, it must turn now to remnants of old pasture, rough grazings and hedgerow banks, looking for wild grasses, legumes and other plants whose genes could be a resource in breeding future herbage species. In livestock, too, concentration on high-input/high-output Continental breeds has all but extinguished many old indigenous breeds and strains which evolved in more stringent conditions and may possess valuable 'fitness' traits such as hardiness and disease resistance. The use of Kerry, Dexter and Irish Maol cattle and Galway sheep is already rewarded under REPS and the genes of indigenous breeds are now likely to be integrated into national livestock breeding programmes.[13]

Global warming and raised levels of carbon dioxide are certain to bring vegetation changes which bear on biodiversity, not least in agriculture. Better grass and clover growth and more haymaking could reduce nitrogen use, produce more insect-friendly swards, and drier silage cuts with less chance of pollution. New forage crops such as maize, fodder beet, lucerne and red clover, new horticultural crops and even southern vineyards will increase the variety of insect habitats and foods – but also problems of pests and weeds which could invite fresh hazards in chemical control. In general, mild wet winters, hot summers and raised carbon dioxide levels should produce a lusher vegetation and increased biodiversity as new insects arrive from continental Europe and new birds take up residence. But they would also bring such changes as the drying out of peatlands into heaths and a rapid growth of bracken and scrub on under-grazed pastures at the margins of farming.[14]

Higher temperatures and CO_2 levels might be expected to benefit Ireland's second great monoculture, the planting of conifers – chiefly Sitka spruce – by the forestry sector. In fact, the final impact is uncertain; there are imponderables such as the spread of defoliating insects and a lack of winter 'chilling' to trigger the normal spring bud-burst. Drier, warmer peatland could boost the growth of forests in the west, but heavier winter rainfall could restrain it.[15]

All this presumes, of course, that warming does not precipitate the regional catastrophe, now seriously proposed, in which a failure of the North Atlantic 'ocean pump' deflects the Gulf Stream away from western Europe, bringing Ireland a winter climate nearer to that of Labrador. What is certain, however, is that reafforestation strategies will continue to arouse debate. Planting proceeds headlong towards a government goal of 17 per cent of land cover (1.2 million hectares) by 2030 – a transformation of landscape on a scale and at a rate unprecedented in the island's history. Most of it is now being done not by the state but by farmers and other private interests. Despite the grants that favour broad-leaved trees and an increased national broadleaf target of 30 per cent adopted in 2000, the great bulk of new forest, including that planted by Coillte, will continue to be of short-rotation conifers from the Pacific coast of North America.

Issues of biodiversity relate less to the trees themselves (though this has its own importance) than to the natural ecosystems they create for the rest of wildlife. Conifer plantations are notorious among nature-lovers as dark forests where no birds sing, but this is not quite true. At the woodland edge they attract a good many ordinary farmland birds, together with a handful of forest specialists twittering high in the canopy. On overgrazed moorland, and in their younger stages, the plantations have actually offered sanctuary to birdlife, if at the cost of displacing some scarce or endangered species such as golden plover and Greenland white-fronted geese.

They also shelter mammals (red squirrel and pine marten among them), and amphibians and insects. While the original spread of conifers across peatland undoubtedly destroyed valuable habitats and plant communities, the plants now fenced in at their margins -heathers, mosses, liverworts – can provide a reservoir of species for repopulating the often devastated commonage outside. Conifer afforestation also smothered 27,000 hectares of old native woodlands, but many of these are now being retrieved under Coillte's new ecological agenda.

Maintaining biodiversity is a key principle of Sustainable Forest Management, the code of forest protection initiated by Europe's environmental ministers in 1993 (the Helsinki Process). Coillte, The Irish Forestry Board, has committed itself to SFM across an estate which includes 15,000 hectares of SACs, 2,000 hectares of 'enhancement and restoration forests', and great areas of unplanted hills, peatland, swamps and lakes. Fifteen per cent of its lands are to be managed with nature conservation, not timber, as the primary objective. [16]

There has been a profound widening of forest values to include biodiversity and ecological concerns in Coillte's management philosophy and structures, and despite the scepticism expressed by some green activists, I am confident that this will be followed through in the company's operations. Just as it has been changing the visual patterns of its forests to harmonise with landscape contours (notably in scenic mountain areas of the west), a similar seriousness is evident towards the new ecological goals. Indeed, the loss of this commitment (and the fact that Coillte owns 440,000 hectares of state land) should be one of the strongest arguments against the sale of Coillte to private commercial interests.

Two-thirds of Coillte's forest stands are now of one species: Sitka spruce or lodgepole pine, neither of which evolved within our native ecosystems. While new plantations on acid soils will introduce mixed species of conifers, the scope for commercial broadleaf timber (as distinct from planting broadleaves for nature conservation or landscape purposes) is greatest on the better land now becoming available under Coillte's Farm Forestry Partnership Scheme. The figure of five per cent broadleaves planted in 1998 shows the very low base from which the company has to advance. The Heritage Council has recommended a national planting target of *equal numbers* of conifers and broadleaved species, citing an EU national average of 60 per cent of broadleaves. To achieve such a radical change, it suggests, Coillte should actually concentrate on broadleaves (such as oak, ash, birch and sycamore), with the future market for high-quality furniture hardwoods in mind.[17]

A mix of species can be achieved in many ways – even in parallel stripes – but the ecological ideal is, of course, a mixture of trees that comes closest to natural forest. Mixing trees within stands (including planting broadleaves among conifers) and felling selectively, at different times, to preserve a continuous woodland cover, is what the Heritage Council would like to see. This approach is echoed in the biodiversity guidelines included in the Code of Best Forest Practice, based on SFM principles and published in 2000 by the government's Forest Service.[18] The ecological thought and care that it prescribes are remarkably thorough (even to the retention of old trees and decomposing deadwood, which support its own special range of beetles and other invertebrates). They represent an ideal match of biodiversity principles with forestry for timber, and abiding by them is now a condition of forest grant-aid.

They serve as a bridge, indeed, between conservation of biodiversity and a 'low-intensity' approach to forestry which reconnects with skills of woodland management long lost to Ireland. Our native woodland was reduced to some three per cent of the island as long ago as 1600, and none of the fragments surviving today can be considered untouched by man: even the most ancient woods hold massive stumps created by oak coppicing, and some, like the venerable and natural-seeming oakwoods of Killarney, were replanted by foresters two centuries ago.

All native woodlands, however, can be seen as reservoirs of biodiversity, preserving the ancient seed stock of native tree species and woodland plants – even of the genes of bluebells, flowering in woods of oak and hazel for many thousands of years. A quite inspiring recognition of their value is the new Native Woodlands Scheme launched by the Forest Service in 2001. Working with Dúchas and other expert woodland groups, the scheme will give substantial grants to the restoration of 15,000 hectares of native broadleaved woodland in private hands, and the planting of as much new woodland with native species. The emphasis is on conservation: fences to keep out sheep and cattle, clearance of rhododendron, coppicing to let in the light. Only the most depleted of woods will be replanted, with a mix of native trees, and even these will have to be planned as low-intensity forestry, with selective felling and continuous cover. The woodlands will include 1,000 hectares of riparian trees (replacing, very often, those felled by angling interests). These riverbank woods will become new wildlife corridors for birds and mammals.

To show how native woodlands should be managed and restored was part of the purpose of the 'People's Millennium Forests' project, launched in 2000 and managed by Coillte. It has planted more than a million trees to restore eight native woodlands to their old diversity and create eight new ones with a full mix of native species. In some of them, broadleafed trees will be grown for timber by the 'close-to-nature' silviculture just described. In the SAC oak woodlands, however, ecological integrity extends to planting only with seedlings raised from acorns collected by voluntary groups in or around the woods, and this kind of scrupulousnesss is promised also in the Native Woodlands Scheme.[19]

The new attention to our surviving native woods should help defend them from the county council road engineers, so readily attracted in their designs to stretches of local woodland. But for some Irish naturalists, the ideal, one-off Millennium memorial would have been a large 'people's forest' – one big enough to get lost in – planted in the midlands on land bought by the government, and then left alone to grow. The cost of one national sports stadium would, indeed, have paid for a very sizeable new native forest, to support the recreational enthusiasm of a great many fans of nature.

The Forest Service lies, however, within the Department of Communications, Marine and Natural Resources. Here there is, inevitably, an uneasy partnership between the urge to exploit and the need to conserve in the harness of 'sustainable development'. As commercial fish stocks dwindle around our coasts, fish-farm cages ride the waves of every sheltered inlet. Out on the horizon, hired survey ships map the geology of the seabed, part of a considerable investment in marine research. The department's knowledge of what is sustainable in its primary sector, the ocean, is still incredibly scanty. Unlike the exploitation of natural resources on land, each new step in marine development depends on the initiative, expertise and ecological ethics of working scientists. To a degree unique in history, they have come to mediate human intrusion on the sea.

Scientific assessment of fish stocks has been used, often with great political resistance, to slow the collapse of traditional food species. As these decline under the pressure of (mainly continental) fishing fleets, or struggle to keep their populations above safe biological limits, more and more of the fishing effort is aimed at new, deep-water species. As a group these are naturally long-lived, growing very slowly and reproducing late, so that trawlers can take more fish in a short time than the species can replace. Almost nothing is known of the population dynamics of such remote and unfamiliar fish, and even less of their role in deep, cold ecosystems where change comes dropping slow. Their sustainable management is 'particularly difficult' according to the Oslo-Paris Commission (OSPAR), which monitors the health of the Northeast Atlantic. Yet Irish trawlers join those from France, Spain, Norway and Scotland in taking huge hauls (50,000 tonnes in 1999) from the waters west of Ireland, and Irish scientists have been among the most enthusiastic in assessing the food quality of the new, deep-water species and helping to bring them to market.

The discovery in the Porcupine, Seabight and Rockall troughs of spectacular cold-water coral reefs – 'city hubs' of deep-water biodiversity – has brought urgent research: reefs like these have been badly battered by bottom-trawling, to which must now be added the steady advance of oil and gas exploration and the prospect of undersea mining. Some 200,000 square kilometres of continental shelf and its teeming marine life are presented as a new frontier of prosperity. The state's investment in research by the Marine Institute and Geological Survey of Ireland is devoted first to potential exploitation and second to the ecological parameters that may set limits to it.

Marine biologists still have so far to go in understanding the myriad ecosystems and life strategies of the oceans that few of them need urging towards the 'precautionary principle' – the informed prudence that refuses to dice with possibly disastrous outcomes. But the personal 'frontier' excitement of their field is, understandably, readily harnessed to new, entrepreneurial inshore projects.

As one example, the west coast's millions of tonnes of wrack and kelp have been marked out afresh as a natural resource for extraction of alginate chemicals, widely used in food processing.[20] The harvesting of seaweeds can clearly be sustainable in terms of regrowth, but this has to be balanced with their living value to the inshore ecosystem. They give food, physical support and shelter to a great diversity of animals and plants; even their particles and trace elements are vital to inshore biochemistry.

Similarly, the great west coast deposits of calcareous red algae known as maerl, lying in beds measured in millions of tonnes, have a potential market as a lime-rich soil dressing and for other uses. But, as research for the Marine Institute makes clear, the beds are a rare habitat, a virtually non-renewable resource that hosts a rich diversity of animals and plants. The role of maerl in the inshore ecosystem clearly needs much more investigation. [21]

At more than 7,500 kilometres, the much-indented Irish coastline seems to offer plenty of room for even the trebling of coastal fish-farming and shellfish mariculture to which the government is now committed. But siting operations to allow a proper coexistence with nature immediately changes the picture. Not surprisingly, the inshore waters with the richest natural ecosystems are also the most productive for mariculture, so that many of the bays now proposed as SACs are already supporting salmon cages and shellfish culture. How much mariculture is too much? How is the unacceptable impact of a fish-farm to be defined? What will be the human impact on the predatory attentions of seals, cormorants and herons, and how can this be squared with goals of conservation? [22]

The protection of grey seals under the Wildlife Act, and the steady rise in the adjoining UK populations have not helped the traditional conflict between the animals and fishermen. Arguments about the seals' share and what it does to fish stocks are complex when discussed in scientific and economic terms, and research continues to resist such crude solutions as culling. Indeed, a new Irish-Welsh study insists that, before any 'sustainable management' strategies are possible, research must deal with the Irish Sea as an entire ecosystem, with the seals as just one dynamic element living and feeding within it. [23]

Ireland's responsibility for marine mammals took a leap into the blue when in 1991 the national waters, extending 200 miles from the coast, were declared a whale and dolphin sanctuary, with a total ban on hunting – the first such sanctuary in Europe. This may have been a 'green' political gesture, with no immediately obvious economic consequences, but it has brought real responsibilities of research and management. Substantial numbers of dolphins and harbour porpoises, for example, are caught accidentally in gillnets in the Celtic Sea, and ways are now being sought to warn them away.

The 'discovery' of the sea that overtook Ireland in the final decades of the twentieth century has drawn an island people into a whole new interface with the natural world: an adventure popularly shared in new aquariums and the glimpses of marine life on television. There is a legitimate excitement to all this, and to the new explorations funded by the state and commercial interests, but, for most people, the strangeness and remoteness of the undersea world give it a secondhand reality.

The EU-funded BioMAR project of 1992–1996 included the largest field survey of seashore and seabed ever conducted in Ireland.[24] It provided basic data for marine conservation and marked out zones of specially rich diversity. The Republic's only Marine Reserve is the landlocked, though remarkable, Lough Hyne in County Cork, and the new survey prompted ideas of undersea equivalents of national parks or wilderness areas in locations like the Blasket and Skellig Islands in County Kerry or the Saltees in Co Wexford. Marine national parks have grown in importance on the global conservation scene, and even commercial users of marine resources are beginning to see the virtues of sanctuary areas free from exploitation. The sea probably now provides the greatest scope for new national parks, and no doubt this century's technology will provide the wider means of enjoying them. Ultimately, the protection of nursery zones for fish and the protection of especially rich ecosystems as underwater marine parks, could create a partnership of tourism and local fishing. The extent to which Ireland can tailor marine development to small-scale local enterprise may be the ultimate test of its sustainability.

Meanwhile, the concentration is on the designation of marine SACs, ranging from open water to saltmarshes and cliffs. Like their inland equivalents, they are protected by 'notifiable actions' which need ministerial consent, ranging from jet ski hire and dolphin-watching tours to fishing with nets or commercial winkle-picking. At the start of 2001, however, Dúchas had the services of a single marine scientist to help its conservation rangers in monitoring marine SACs from the north of Donegal to the bays of Kerry and Cork.

Inevitably, an air of improvisation and aspiration still hangs over much of the new conservation fabric of designations, frameworks and guidelines. Few impacts of our European Union membership have been as far-reaching as the insistence on concern for nature, or are linking so many separate agencies into a network of mutual consultation and support. The process has also shown up some critical gaps.

Appraising the natural heritage in its *Ireland's Environment: A Millennium Report*, the Environmental Protection Agency concluded simply: 'It has not been possible, except in general terms, to assess Ireland's biodiversity. We do not know precisely what it entails. Inadequate data is a serious problem.... Furthermore, in the Republic of Ireland there is no biological records centre... essential if species diversity is to be properly monitored.' [25]

The very baseline of conservation seemed to have been lost from view – that of knowing exactly what species we have and how they are distributed. In the 1970s, amateur naturalists and schoolchildren joined professional biologists in recording the country's wildlife species for the Irish Biological Records Centre. This was set up in 1971 by An Foras Forbartha, our first conservation research agency, but its existence became obscured in the subsequent political shuffling of conservation functions.

The new National Parks and Wildlife Service (now included in Dúchas), with research priorities largely set by Europe, mounted ad hoc inventories and surveys of rare or threatened habitats, plants and animals. But this is not quite the centrally integrated, ever-expanding, computer-friendly inventory of Ireland's biodiversity that the EPA has in mind. In 2002, the Heritage Council was urging its own detailed and costed proposals for a National Biological Records Centre.

While conservation research has indeed become highly professional, it would be wrong to suggest that the NPWS has neglected the potential of skill and effort in the enthusiastic amateur. Its field staff have fully supported, for example, the enthusiasts of BirdWatch Ireland in the national monitoring of waterbirds wintering in the estuaries and wetlands and the breeding birds of the countryside – both critical surveys at a time of rapid coastal construction and agricultural transition. Now, even the original interactive nature of the Irish Biological Records Centre has reappeared, I am pleased to see, in the new handbook of Irish mammals commissioned by Dúchas: 'If you have records of any Irish mammals, the following two organisations would be delighted to hear from you . . .'[26]

Bracketed there with the Irish Biological Records Centre at Dúchas is its Northern Ireland equivalent: CeDAR, the Centre for Environmental Data and Recording, founded by the Ulster Museum in Belfast in 1995.[27] It can already boast of more than a million species records, and a network of local recorders in statutory agencies, wildlife and conservation organisations or working as individual amateur naturalists. Some of the records are 'sensitive' (exact breeding locations for rare birds, for example) and are kept confidential, but ready computer access by the public is part of CeDAR's mission of offering people the knowledge of their local natural history. In 2000, CeDAR, with support from Dúchas, launched a four-year, island-wide survey of dragonfly species. It was rewarded, in its first summer, with quite startling records of three species new to Ireland, discovered by bird-watchers at the lakes and lagoons of County Wexford.

Our biodiversity stretches almost infinitely beyond the birds, plants, insects and animals familiar or even visible to the average countrylover. In the lists of the Biodiversity Plan, as prepared by Dúchas, are many species, included for their European rarity or ecological importance, which mean very little to the non-scientist. Their protection could set further limitations on the uses of particular patches of land or sea. Thus, the structures of conservation make considerable demands on trust: on the one hand, that the process is necessary to some ideal balance of nature, if not actual human survival; on the other, that it is being carried through wholeheartedly and efficiently. In Ireland, we have not quite achieved the ring of conviction. Too much of what is promised still seems too good to be true, especially for 'green' activists long schooled in disillusion. But the steady permeation of biodiversity principles, together with the money to put them into effect, is releasing the enthusiasm of many well-motivated people at key levels of the public service.

Ireland's geological history, caught up in great crustal events, has left us an island of wonderfully varied terrain. On the continents of the world, there are forests and plains and deserts that roll on for ever, but this small island offers change at each new turn in the road: change, too, in weather, hour by hour. We did not do so well, however, in the variety of species in nature's restocking of the island as the ice finally withdrew 10,000 years ago. As one of the last parts of Europe to be recolonised by flora and fauna, and isolated by the rising post-glacial sea, we have acquired only roughly two-thirds of the insects that Britain has (which still leaves us with about 16,000 species) only about half the mammals and about two-thirds as many native plants.

Along with our more obvious treasures, such as an abundance of choughs and otters, and celebrated European rarities like the Kerry spotted slug, we also have a richness in such unconsidered species as communities of ferns, mosses and liverworts, some of which remain to be discovered in the moister niches of woodland and moor. As an artist of sorts I find their forms and textures exquisite: well worth a wet knee on the bog or a splash from a waterfall to get a closer look. The 'lowest' plants can be so intricately fashioned, as if by a patient jeweller, yet every twist of a leaf has a purpose perfectly matched to habitat. In 1999, four rare liverworts and fourteen rare mosses were granted a special Flora Protection Order. Among them, prompted by the EU Habitats Directive, was a liverwort called petalwort, *Petalophyllum ralfsii*, which turns out to grow in abundant patches in the dunes on the shore below me. I had never noticed it, and no wonder: even a botanist must learn to pick it out on the ground, and its tiny rosette, with translucent wings a single cell thick, is best enjoyed under a microscope.

Liverworts and (even 'lower') algae, growing on the surface of the bog, help to stop it drying out and hold the peat together; perhaps petalwort, too, has an equally significant effect. But to say what species *do* is not to say what they are *for*. Imputing purpose to nature is the sin of teleology, and perhaps the hardest thing is to demand neither beauty nor purpose from biodiversity, even when it overflows with both.

Outside my window as I write, on a chilly day in February, goldfinches and house-sparrows fight for a place on the nut-feeder in the hedge. I am thrilled by the goldfinches, with their bright-red masks and vivid yellow wing-patches: the clean country sparrows are quite outshone. Yet, watching the birds together, I am just as glad to see the sparrows, ubiquitous street-birds of my childhood. They are versatile seed-eaters, thriving in the spilled-grain era of the horse, but they need to feed their young on insects — and these, it seems, are now vanishing from urban heartlands. The decline of city sparrows is a message about change. The decline of any species is a message about change — the grouse that calls for the heatherless hills, the ice-age snail for an ancient marsh, drained and built on. We often cheat about the rarities that move us with their plight, insisting that they charm us in some way: we have to learn a less self-centred view.

But the glorious goldfinches, too, have a point to make. In the lean years of the Irish Free State, they were greatly preyed upon by men who boiled up holly-bark to make bird-lime and poured it like treacle over bushes and thistleheads. They called the finches down with decoys and later dispatched them, in cages, to England, in company with siskins, skylarks and linnets. The Protection of Wild Birds Act 1930 put such exports beyond the law, much to the disquiet of the young Dáil Deputy for Dublin South, Seán Lemass. The Act, he said, would bring greater misery to the 300 people who made a precarious living in the bird-catching trade. 'If the economic situation becomes better, we can then afford to indulge in luxury legislation of this kind, but we must put the necessities of human beings before those of wild birds.'

Seventy years on, the economic situation is unimaginably better, built on foundations that Lemass helped to lay in the 1960s, and what has become important in the conservation of birds is not (with some exceptions) protection from bird-catchers and egg-collectors, but guaranteeing their habitats and food supplies. As more and more of the Earth's surface is taken up by people and their demands (which, for very many in the West, go rapaciously beyond their needs), the rest of nature is forced to shrink away.

On our small island, 'sustainable development' will be very much about space: the literal sprawl of concrete across the landscape and the consequential human impact upon nature. Already, our 'ecological footprint' – the measure of national consumption as it uses up natural resources – is more than three times our fair global share. The planet's total biologically productive area works out at roughly two hectares per person, allowing a grudging 12 per cent of Earth for all the other species.

The 'footprint' of the average Irish person already covers almost six hectares, on a level with Sweden and more than half a hectare ahead of the people in Britain. [28]

The rapid expansion in Ireland's footprint should surprise nobody. It is part of a global trend, but also, of course, special to the velvet spoor of the Celtic tiger, ravenous for imported resources and luxuries. In the past, a low population density and a high proportion of productive farmland meant that we trod relatively lightly on the Earth. Now, our soaring demands not only impinge directly on foreign fields and forests, mines and oil wells, but we also add to the ecological costs of energy and pollution in other countries – the chimneys are smoking somewhere else.

A comfortably dispersed population and a heavy reliance on imports has spared Ireland much of the true ecological cost of living in the developed world. Any significant leap in the island's population, climbing already towards 5.5 million, will make it even more difficult to leave room for nature within the physical fabric of our lives. This essay was completed as discussion began on the implications of discoveries about the human genome: notably that people are far more responsive to their environment than to the exclusive dictates of any exceptional number of genes. We start out, it seems, with much the same genetic complexity as any other mammal. For me, as, I am sure, for many 'deep ecologists', this seemed to confirm the need to preserve our own links with nature and thus to avoid constructing human ecosystems which produce unhappiness, violence and crime.

REFERENCES

1. E.O.Wilson. *The Diversity of Life.* London:Allen Lane, (1992) p. 158.
2. J.E. Lovelock. *Gaia:A New Look at Life on Earth.* Oxford University Press (1979).
3. Green 2000 Advisory Group Report to the Taoiseach, 1993, p. 292.
4. First National Report on the Implementation of the Convention on Biological Diversity by Ireland, 1998. Department of Arts, Heritage, Gaeltacht and the Islands, p. 73.
5. T.C.Aughney and M.J. Gormally. 'Farm Habitats in Annaghdown, County Galway: Management Practices in the 1940s'. Environmental Science Unit, NUI Galway (1999).
6. R. Douthwaite. 'The small farm in Ireland – crisis and opportunity'. *Ceide*: 4 (4), 5-8 (2001). Also *Short Circuit* (Resurgence, 1996).
7. Sustainable Development: A Strategy for Ireland. Department of the Environment, 1997.
8. See, for example, Jeremy Purseglove *Taming the Flood*, Oxford University Press (1988).
9. 'Protecting important natural areas in Ireland: 30 years of progress'. Paper delivered to RIA symposium on landscape history. 27 October 2000.
10. J.A. Good. 'The potential role of ecological corridors for habitat conservation in Ireland: a review'. Dúchas: Irish Wildlife Manuals No. 2 (1998). See also the website: *www.econetireland. net/*
11. See 7 above, p.107.
12. First National Report on the Implementation of the Convention on Biological Diversity by Ireland. DAHGI 1988, p.106.
13. *ibid*, pp. 82-83.
14. Climate Change: Studies on the Implications for Ireland. Department of the Environment, 1991: 4-44.
15. *ibid*, pp. 45-68.
16. Coillte's Forests:A Framework for Sustainable Forest Management. Coillte, 1999.
17. Policy Paper on Forestry and the National Heritage.The Heritage Council, 1999.
18. *Forest Biodiversity Guidelines* is available separately from the Forest Service, Department of Communications, Marine and Natural Resources.

19. D. Hickie. *Native Trees and Forests of Ireland*. Dublin: Gill & Macmillan, (2002).

20. National Seaweed Forum Report. Department of the Marine and Natural Resources (2000).

21. A Study of Selected Maerl Beds in Irish Waters and their Potential for Sustainable Extraction. Marine Institute, 1999.

22. M.L. Heffernan. 'A review of the ecological implications of mariculture and intertidal harvesting in Ireland.' Dúchas: Irish Wildlife Manuals No. 7 (1999).

23. O. Kiely et al. 'Grey Seals: Status and Monitoring in the Irish and Celtic Seas'. Maritime Ireland/Wales INTERREG Report No. 3 (2000).

24. BioMar Biotope Viewer (CD). Environmental Sciences Unit, Trinity College, Dublin, 1997.

25. L. Stapleton, M. Lehane, and P. Toner, (eds). *Ireland's Environment: A Millennium Report*. Environmental Protection Agency (2000), p. 181.

26. T. Hayden and R. Harrington. *Exploring Irish Mammals*. Dublin: Town House (2000).

27. Available from: *www.ulstermuseum.org.uk/cedar*

28. Available from: *www.ecouncil.ac.cr/rio/focus/report/english/footprint/*